ideals
EASTER

Vol. 46, No. 2

Publisher, Patricia A. Pingry
Executive Editor, Cynthia Wyatt
Art Director, Patrick McRae
Production Manager, Jeff Wyatt
Editorial Assistant, Kathleen Gilbert
Copy Editors, Marian Hollyday
                 Rhonda Colburn

ISBN 0-8249-1070-2

IDEALS—Vol. 46, No.2 March 1989 IDEALS (ISSN 0019-137X) is published eight times a year: February, March, April, June, August, September, November, December by IDEALS PUBLISHING CORPORATION, Nelson Place at Elm Hill Pike, Nashville, Tenn. 37214. Second class postage paid at Nashville, Tennessee, and additional mailing offices. Copyright © 1989 by IDEALS PUBLISHING CORPORA-TION. POSTMASTER: Send address changes to Ideals, Post Office Box 148000, Nashville, Tenn. 37214-8000. All rights reserved. Title IDEALS registered U.S. Patent Office.

SINGLE ISSUE—$3.95
ONE-YEAR SUBSCRIPTION—eight consecutive issues as published—$17.95
TWO-YEAR SUBSCRIPTION—sixteen consecutive issues as published—$31.95
Outside U.S.A., add $6.00 per subscription year for postage and handling.

ACKNOWLEDGMENTS

IF MY BARK SINK and A LIGHT EXISTS IN SPRING by Emily Dickinson were reprinted by permission of the pub-lishers and the Trustees of Amherst College from *THE POEMS OF EMILY DICKINSON*, Thomas H. Johnson, ed., Cambridge, Mass.: The Belknap Press of Harvard University Press, Copyright 1951, © 1955, 1979, 1983 by the President and Fellows of Harvard College; BEFORE STORM from *POOL IN THE MEADOW* by Frances Frost. Copyright 1933 by Frances M. Frost. Reprinted by permission of Houghton Mifflin Company; RAIN and SPRING MEADOW were re-printed from *THE EVERLASTING MINUTE AND OTHER LYRICS* by Louis Ginsberg. Copyright 1937 by Liveright Pub-lishing Corporation. With permission of the publisher, Liveright Publishing Corporation; THE MASTER from *THE FRIENDLY WAY* by Edgar A. Guest. Copyright 1931 by The Reilly & Lee Co. Used by permission; YOUNG THINGS by Arthur Guiterman from *DEATH AND GENERAL PUTNAM*, Copyright 1935 by E.P. Dutton and renewed 1969 by Louise H. Sclove. Reprinted by permission of Louise H. Sclove; IVAN'S EASTER SERVICE from *THE OBSERVANCE OF EASTER* by Amelia W. Swayne. Used by permission of Friends General Conference (FGC) 1520–B Race Street, Philadelphia, PA 19102. All rights reserved; excerpt from *HOW TO BE HAPPY THOUGH HUMAN* by W. Beran Wolfe, M.D. Copyright 1931 by W. Beran Wolfe and renewed 1959 by Florence Wolfe. Reprinted by permission of Henry Holt and Co., Inc. Our sincere thanks to the following whose addresses we were unable to locate: Dr. Martin T. Bergsjo for APRIL FOOLING from *A POCKET FULL OF WRY;* the Estate of Anne Campbell for IN THE GARDEN; the Estate of Inez Marrs for INDISPUTABLE EVIDENCE; Dorene for HOMEBUILDER; Don Thorne for TO A CHIPMUNK.

Inside front cover by John Gadja

Inside back cover by Armont Hyde, Jr.

Front and back covers by Gene Ahrens

A Light Exists in Spring

Emily Dickinson

A light exists in spring
   Not present on the year
At any other period.
   When March is scarcely here

A color stands abroad
   On solitary hills
That science cannot overtake
   But human nature *feels.*

It waits upon the lawn;
   It shows the furthest tree
Upon the furthest slope we
     know;
   It almost speaks to me.

Then, as horizons step,
   Or noons report away,
Without the formula of
     sound,
   It passes, and we stay:

A quality of loss
   Affecting our content,
As trade had suddenly
     encroached
   Upon a sacrament.

Photo Overleaf
PARK NEAR LISSE
HOLLAND
M. Thonig
H. Armstrong Roberts, Inc.

Photo Opposite
FLORAL SPLENDOR
Ken Dequaine, Photographer

The Butterfly

Alice Freeman Palmer

I hold you at last in my hand,
Exquisite child of the air.
Can I ever understand
How you grew to be so fair?

You came to my linden tree
To taste its delicious sweet,
I sitting here in the shadow and shine
Playing around its feet.

Now I hold you fast in my hand,
You marvelous butterfly,
Till you help me to understand
The eternal mystery.

From that creeping thing in the dust
To this shining bliss in the blue!
God give me courage to trust
I can break my chrysalis too!

Photo Opposite
BUTTERFLY AND MARIGOLDS
Monserrate J. Schwartz

Indisputable Evidence

Inez Marrs

In the blaze of crimson sunsets
And the pastel dew of dawn,
In chocolate clods of earth
And every chartreuse lawn;

In the trees' bud-swollen branches
And dandelions' lace,
In hyacinths' obeisance
And tulips' erect grace;

In every lilac cluster
And sprig of mignonette,
In each intrepid crocus
And timid violet;

In pink-fringed apple blossoms
And the pansies' playful faces,
In dogwoods' pearly whiteness
And magenta redbud laces;

In every fragile rosebud
And hardy wayside bloom,
In the Easter lilies' promise
Of life beyond the tomb;

Spring once more has come to earth,
There's proof in nature's art,
But better proof I have within,
Where spring is in my heart.

Photo Opposite
PANSIES
SHORE ACRES STATE PARK, OREGON
Ed Cooper, Photographer

DAFFODILS

Karen Olsen Coy

As I gaze upon the maze
Of golden yellow daffodils,
I pick a few to bring to you
To place upon your window sills.

Dainty, neat, and oh, so sweet,
They lift one's spirits way up high;
They are able to grace a table
And cheer up people dropping by.

Oh, how bright! They just delight
Me 'cause they look so bright and gay:
Yellow, sunny, sweet as honey,
Pretty as a new spring day.

I can sing, "Oh, welcome, spring!"
And shout it o'er the fields and hills;
But in my heart right from the start
I'm looking for the daffodils.

Photo Overleaf
CHERRY BLOSSOMS
WASHINGTON MONUMENT
WASHINGTON, D.C.
Tom Till, Photographer

Yearning for Spring

J. Marshall Porter

I'll walk old logging trails when dogwoods bloom
For spring's parade in raiment pearly white.
I'll kneel to catch arbutus' sweet perfume,
And gaze through floating leaves to heavens bright.

I'll hear spring's breezes sighing in the pines
And breathe their fragrance as they pass me by.
I'll bend to watch the bees on columbines
And hear the mourning dove's lamenting sigh.

I'll visit coves where sleeping trilliums wait
Among moss covered rocks for warming sun.
I'll go where purple phlox grows tall and straight
And note the sounds of brooklets as they run.

I'll rest a while astride a fallen log
And hear the shrill cries of a flicker hen.
I'll thrill to yelping when my chummy dog
Pursues a feeding woodchuck to her den.

From deep ravines I'll climb to higher ground
And view the valley from a windy knoll.
I'll raise the clustered flowers I have found
And thank God for the peace within my soul.

Photo Opposite
AZALEAS
G. Hampfler
H. Armstrong Roberts, Inc.

Festive Easter Egg Candies

Easter Egg Candies

Makes approximately 60

  1 14.3-ounce box creamy white frosting mix
  5 tablespoons butter, softened
  3 tablespoons all-purpose flour
  1 tablespoon light corn syrup
  1½ tablespoons hot water
  1¼ pounds (approximately) pastel-colored compound coating, melted for dipping

Combine frosting mix, butter, and flour in bowl; set aside. Combine corn syrup and hot water; add to mixture in bowl. Blend with mixer until mixture resembles fine crumbs. Press into a ball with hands. Form into small egg shapes; dip in melted compound coating.

Note: For variety add desired amounts of melted real chocolate, candied fruit, nuts, coconut, flavorings, or food colorings or use another frosting mix flavor.

Chocolate Easter Eggs

Makes 60 to 100

  1 pound confectioners' sugar
  6 ounces semisweet chocolate-flavored compound coating, wafers or pieces, melted
  1 3-ounce package cream cheese, softened
  1 teaspoon vanilla
  2½ to 3 tablespoons hot water
    Dash salt
  2 pounds (approximately) any chocolate-flavored compound coating, melted or real chocolate, tempered
    Candy decorations, optional

Blend ½ pound confectioners' sugar with semisweet chocolate-flavored compound coating, cream cheese, vanilla, hot water, and salt. Work in remaining confectioners' sugar with hands. Form mixture into smooth, round ball; form small eggs. Dip in melted chocolate; decorate, if desired.

Variation

Choco-Peanut Butter Easter Eggs: Divide mixture in half. To one half add 2 tablespoons peanut butter; form into small eggs. Repeat with remaining half or leave plain for basic Chocolate Easter Eggs. Dip in melted chocolate; decorate, if desired.

Cheesy Coconut Easter Eggs

Makes approximately 40

  1 3-ounce package cream cheese, softened
  ½ teaspoon vanilla
  1 pound (approximately) confectioners' sugar
  ¼ cup flaked coconut
    Dash salt
  1 pound (approximately) chocolate-flavored or pastel compound coating, melted

Combine cream cheese and vanilla in bowl. Gradually add confectioners' sugar, coconut, and salt. Mix to consistency that can be easily handled, adding more confectioners' sugar, if necessary. Form candy into eggs; let set approximately 1 hour. Dip into compound coating; let set until firm.

Peanut Butter-Marshmallow Eggs

Makes approximately 80

  1½ cups butter or margarine, softened
  5 to 6 cups sifted confectioners' sugar
  1 cup peanut butter
  1¾ cups marshmallow creme
  2 teaspoons vanilla
  1¾ pounds (approximately) any chocolate-flavored compound coating, melted or real chocolate, tempered

Cream butter and 2 cups confectioners' sugar in large bowl until light and fluffy. Add peanut butter, marshmallow creme, and vanilla; blend well. Gradually add remaining confectioners' sugar; mix to consistency that can be easily handled. Form into egg shapes. Dip eggs in melted chocolate; let stand until firm.

Clockwise, from Top: Chocolate Easter Eggs, Easter Egg Candies, Choco-Peanut Butter Easter Eggs, and Cheesy Coconut Easter Eggs, surrounded by Peanut Butter-Marshmallow Eggs.

The Easter Bunny

Margaret Rorke

Tonight a furry little gent
With big and floppy ears
Will hop his way into the homes
Where childhood still appears.
He's worked all week at dying eggs;
His kitchen is a mess.
The sink is full of pots and pans,
And all is stickiness.

By now he's put his ribbon on,
And started on his way
With baskets that he wove by hand
In colors very gay.
Inside each one some candy chicks
And chocolate rabbits sit
On finely shredded paper grass
Where jellybeans permit.

Behind the chairs and davenports
When Easter's sun shall rise,
The little ones will seek and find
Those gifts with joyful cries.
Back home for now another year,
His trip a great success,
The Easter Bunny still must face
That awful kitchen mess.

Breakfast Time

Ruth Helderman

My back lawn is a breakfast table
With cloth of velvet green,
At which, if I am very still,
A rabbit may be seen.

He nibbles four-leaf clovers,
He hops upon my walk,
Flips morning dew from dampened paws—
How nice if he could talk!

He keeps his furry ears alert
To hear if danger nears;
Then using his paws for a washcloth,
He grooms his face and ears.

It makes a small boy wonder
As he ponders the problem o'er,
Why a bunny gets by with "after,"
But a boy must wash "before"!

Spring Promise

Tender buds on shrub and tree
Boast of Spring's bright victory—
Dormant seeds beneath Earth's floor
Leap from darkness through life's door.

The world has changed its winter scene
To fertile fields with glint of green;
Blossoms burst to meet the sun—
The glad awakening has begun!

Somewhere beneath Death's winter sleep
Mortals too wake from the deep—
For Christ arose that he might bring
His promise of eternal spring!

Iris W. Bray
Reedville, VA

He Arose!

We wonder why it had to be
That Jesus died upon the tree,
    For he was sinless, but he came
    To save us all. Oh, praise his name!
The debt was ours. We could not pay.
He gave his life. We're free today,
    For only God's beloved son
    Could pay the price for everyone.

As dawn was breaking that third day,
God's angel rolled the stone away.
    The Son of God stepped forth in power
    And beauty, for this was his hour.
The Lord of Life indeed was King,
Master now of every thing.
    Oh, praise the Lord, we are forgiven.
    He opened wide the gates of heaven.

Because he is our light, our way,
Death has no sting for us today.
    When Christ arose, somehow I know
    The earth rejoiced and was aglow,
As we must be who love the Lord
With expectation, looking toward
    The time when we his face shall see,
    And live with him eternally.

Alta Richardson McLain
Sebring, FL

Reflections

Love Can Never Die

When you open your heart
It's like a flower blooming.
The beauty soon shines through.
For love, like a flower,
stays in its bud
'til the summer comes,
and then shows off its beauty.
Then it closes up again.
But unlike the flower that dies at
summer's end,
love will last forever.
There is just one part of a person's heart
that will never die.
That is love . . .
Unlike the flower,
Love can never die . . .

Emily S. Downing, age 9
Oneonta, NY

My Divine Guide

I know not the way I am going,
    But well do I know my Guide!
With a childlike faith do I give my hand
    To the mighty Friend by my side.
And the only thing that I say to Him
    As He takes it is, "Hold it fast!
Suffer me not to lose the way,
    And lead me home at last."

Kae Carter Jaworski
Los Angeles, CA

Puddle Jumpers

Little boys are playing
On sidewalks rain-fresh wet,
Hunting out the puddles
They've not waded yet.
Their clothes are soaked and dripping
As they splash the dirty ooze;
And all their toes are squishing
Inside their Sunday shoes.

Ardis Rittenhouse
Alexandria, IN

Readers are invited to submit unpublished, original poetry, short anecdotes, and humorous reflections on life for possible publication in future *Ideals* issues. Please send copies only; manuscripts will not be returned. Writers will receive $10 for each published submission. Send materials to "Readers' Reflections," Ideals Publishing Corporation, P.O. Box 140300, Nashville, Tennessee 37214-0300.

Hunting Easter Eggs

Mabel F. Hill

We will hunt for Easter eggs,
Pretty, colored Easter eggs,
We'll fill our baskets good and full
Early Easter morning.

Fill each basket to the top,
To the top, to the top.
When it's full then you must stop
Early Easter morning.

Hunting Easter eggs is fun,
Lots of fun, loads of fun.
We'll find eggs for everyone,
Early Easter morning.

Young Things

Arthur Guiterman

Dappled fawns on hills and holts,
Quaint and leggy calves and colts,
Pups and kittens soft as silk,
Full of innocence and milk,

Lambs and kids, a sportive crew,
Downy chicks and ducklings too,
Cubs in roly-poly glee,
Babies gurgling pink and wee,

Children, mostly under seven—
   Of such is the kingdom of heaven.

CRAFTWORKS

Materials Needed:

Sugar Egg:

   5 cups granulated sugar
   1 slightly beaten egg white
Hard plastic 6-inch egg mold with a flat
    bottom
Hard plastic mold for bunny figures (These
    can be purchased in craft shops.)
2 *or* 3 pieces 8-inch square cardboard
Bowl, spoon, knife, spatula, damp cloth

Decorative Icing:

   3 egg whites
   4 cups confectioners' sugar
  ½ teaspoon cream of tartar
Food coloring
Decorator bags
Assorted decorator tips
Small candy pieces for interior "garden"
Electric mixer and bowl

Step One: Preparing Sugar Mixture

Place 5 cups sugar and 1 slightly beaten egg white in a bowl. Mix by hand until the sugar feels like wet sand. The mixture should pack easily. Keep covered with a damp cloth if not used immediately.

Step Two: Making Your Egg

Pack sugar mixture firmly into both halves of the plastic mold. Scrape off any excess sugar with a spatula so that the top is level. Place a piece of cardboard over the top and flip the mold upside down. Lift the mold away carefully and set aside. If you are using a plastic mold for figures to place inside your egg, make them with the sugar mixture that you have left.

For the viewing hole, make a straight vertical cut 1½ inches from the smaller end of the top and bottom halves of the egg. Leave the separated pieces in position rather than discarding them. This allows the egg to dry evenly, which will make hollowing it out easier.

Step Three: Drying and Preparing the Egg for Decorating

Dry your egg in a preheated 200° oven for 3 to 6 minutes, or allow it to air dry for 2 to 3 hours. Also dry the small sugar figures. These can be dried in the oven, but watch them to make sure they do not turn brown.

When the egg halves are dry, discard the small pieces from the ends. Carefully lift each half and use a spoon to scoop out the insides until you have a shell that is ½ inch to ¼ inch thick. Place the halves hollow side up on cardboard and allow them to dry again in a 200° oven for 1 to 2 minutes.

Step Four: Preparing the Icing

In a mixing bowl combine 3 egg whites, 4 cups confectioners' sugar, and ½ teaspoon cream of tartar. Beat at high speed for 7 to 10 minutes. Divide the icing into separate portions and add desired food coloring.

Step Five: Decorating the Egg

Using assorted tips on your decorator bag (or wax paper funnels, if preferred), decorate the inside of the bottom portion of the sugar egg with icing to resemble grass, water, trees, etc. . . . Next place your figures and candy in the scene. If figures will not stand, place a dollop of icing behind them.

Photo Opposite
Nancy Robinson

Decorate the top portion of the egg with clouds or continue a tree from the bottom up onto the top.

Step Six: Finishing Your Panoramic Egg

Run a thin line of icing around the rim of the bottom half of the egg. Be careful not to use too much icing or it will flow out onto the outer and inner surfaces when the two halves are joined. Place the top half onto the bottom, matching front flat edges and side seams.

Decorate the seam and the front edge with icing. Decorate the top of the egg with candy or flowers and leaves of icing.

To store your egg until Easter, place it in a paper bag, then put it in a cardboard box. Keep in the least humid area of the house.

Claudette Tidwell

Claudette Tidwell makes wedding cakes and confections for special occasions in Nashville, Tennessee, and is the owner of Cake Creations by Claudette, Inc.

BITS &

Hot Cross Buns . . .

In England the most notable Good Friday custom is the baking of hot cross buns, which are almost universally eaten for breakfast on Good Friday morning. These are buns, or spiced rolls, round in shape, with a cross indented in the top. The custom is said to have originated in 1361 at St. Alban's Abbey, when one of the monks baked them as gifts for the poor.

All kinds of beliefs prevail as to the curative properties of the Good Friday buns. Unlike common bread, they are supposed not to grow moldy when kept, and stale buns are retained for all kinds of purposes—for grating into medicines, as charms against shipwreck, as a means of keeping rats out of the corn, and as a general "good luck" talisman for the household, to be hung from the ceiling on a string.

Alan W. Watts

Excerpt from EASTER: Its Story and Meaning *by Alan W. Watts. Copyright 1950 by Harper & Row, Publishers, Inc. Reprinted by permission of Harper & Row, Publishers, Inc.*

Thank God every morning when you get up that you have something to do that day which must be done, whether you like it or not. Being forced to work, and forced to do your best will breed in you temperance and self-control, diligence and strength of will, cheerfulness and content, and a hundred virtues which the idle will never know.

Charles Kingsley

Beneath these fruit tree boughs that shed
Their snow-white blossoms on my head,
With brightest sunshine round me spread
Of spring's unclouded weather,
In this sequestered nook how sweet
to sit upon my orchard-seat,
And birds and flowers once more to greet,
My last year's friends together.

William Wordsworth

We must love men ere they will seem to us worthy of our love.

William Shakespeare

26

PIECES

Flowers are the sweetest things that God ever made and forgot to put a soul into.

H. W. Beecher

Spring unlocks the flowers to paint the laughing soil.

Reginald Heber

So then the year is repeating its old story again. We are come once more, thank God! to its most charming chapter. The violets and the May flowers are as its inscriptions or vignettes. It always makes a pleasant impression on us, when we open again at these pages of the book of life.

Johann Wolfgang Von Goethe

Reflect upon your present blessings, of which every man has many; not on your past misfortunes, of which all men have some.

Charles Dickens

Blessed be the hand that prepares a pleasure for a child, for there is no saying when and where it may bloom forth.

Douglas Jerrold

All things therefore are charged with love, are charged with God and if we know how to touch them give off sparks and take fire, yield drops and flow, ring and tell of Him.

Gerard Manley Hopkins

This is the world of seeds, of causes, and of tendencies; the other is the world of harvests and results and of perfected and eternal consequences.

Joseph Addison

If we want to know what happiness is we must seek it, not as if it were a pot of gold at the end of the rainbow, but among human beings who are living richly and fully the good life. If you observe a really happy man you will find him building a boat, writing a symphony, educating his son, growing double dahlias in his garden. He will not be searching for happiness as if it were a collar button that has rolled under the radiator. He will have become aware that he is happy in the course of living twenty-four crowded hours of the day.

W. Beran Wolfe

African Violets

Freda V. Fisher

I stand in awe, looking at all
    the flowers on my window shelf,
and realize just how little praise
    that I can claim for self.
Oh yes, I planted every pot;
    I watered, fed, and tended—
but God ordained the rainbow hues;
    the colors He has blended.
I cannot make one leaf to curl,
    or one grow long or rounded.
The blossoms are His lovely gift;
    I stand amazed, astounded.

Photo Opposite
SPRING FLOWERS WITH AFRICAN VIOLETS
Fred Sieb Photography

In the Garden

Anne Campbell

We kneel to plant a garden,
And though we may not pray,
With hope and faith our planting
Will grace a summer day.

We pat the earth upholding
The stalk that pledges bloom,
And thoughts flower, and an image
Of beauty steals the gloom.

We kneel to plant a garden,
And with no thought of prayer,
Our faith pervades the garden
And puts the blossoms there.

April Fooling

Dr. Martin T. Bergsjo

These are the days
Of spring supreme
When the sun pours down
And gardeners scheme
And man released
From winter's brake,
Steps out in the sun
With hoe and rake.

His spirit soars,
He heaves a sigh,
And sees great things
In his mind's eye.
For never in this world
Has been
Such grass as in our dreams
Is seen,
And never flowers
Even rare,
Can with those in the mind
Compare.

April blossoms
With such ease
The world becomes
A gardener's tease.
Comes May, and weeds,
And bugs, and tools.
And then we know
How April fools.

The Last Supper

Now when the even was come, he sat down with the twelve. . . . And as they were eating, Jesus took bread, and blessed it, and brake it, and gave it to the disciples, and said, Take, eat; this is my body. And he took the cup, and gave thanks, and gave it to them, saying, Drink ye all of it; For this is my blood of the new testament, which is shed for many for the remission of sins. But I say unto you, I will not drink henceforth of this fruit of the vine, until that day when I drink it new with you in my Father's kingdom.

Matthew 26:20-29

A new commandment I give unto you, That ye love one another; as I have loved you, that ye also love one another. By this shall all men know that ye are my disciples, if ye have love one to another.

John 13:34-35

I am the true vine, and my Father is the husbandman . . . and every branch that beareth fruit, he purgeth it, that it may bring forth more fruit. . . . Herein is my Father glorified, that ye bear much fruit; so shall ye be my disciples. . . .

If ye keep my commandments, ye shall abide in my love; even as I have kept my Father's commandments, and abide in his love. These things have I spoken unto you, that joy might remain in you, and that your joy might be full.

John 15:1-11

Peace I leave with you, my peace I give unto you: not as the world giveth, give I unto you. Let not your heart be troubled, neither let it be afraid.

John 14:27

The Crucifixion

Pilate said unto them, Whom will ye that I release unto you? Barabbas, or Jesus which is called Christ? For he knew that for envy they had delivered him. When he was set down on the judgment seat, his wife sent unto him, saying, Have thou nothing to do with that just man: for I have suffered many things this day in a dream because of him.

Matthew 27:17-19

All we like sheep have gone astray; we have turned every one to his own way; and the Lord hath laid on him the iniquity of us all. . . . He is brought as a lamb to the slaughter. . . .

Isaiah 53:6-7

And they clothed him with purple, and platted a crown of thorns, and put it about his head, and began to salute him, Hail, King of the Jews! . . . And when they had mocked him, they took off the purple from him, and put his own clothes on him, and led him out to crucify him.

Mark 15:17-20

And it was about the sixth hour, and there was a darkness over all the earth until the ninth hour. And the sun was darkened, and the veil of the temple was rent in the midst. And when Jesus had cried with a loud voice, he said, Father, into thy hands I commend my spirit: and having said thus, he gave up the ghost. Now when the centurion saw what was done, he glorified God, saying, Certainly this was a righteous man.

Luke 23:44-47

But he was wounded for our transgressions, he was bruised for our iniquities: the chastisement of our peace was upon him; and with his stripes we are healed.

Isaiah 53:5

He Is Not Dead

From "Adonais"

Percy Bysshe Shelley

Peace, peacc! hc is not dead, he doth not sleep—
He hath awakened from the dream of life—
'Tis we who, lost in stormy visions, keep
With phantoms an unprofitable strife. . . .

* * *

He has outsoared the shadow of our night;
Envy and calumny, and hate and pain,
And that unrest which men miscall delight,
Can touch him not, and torture not again. . . .

* * *

The One remains, the many change and pass;
Heaven's light forever shines, Earth's shadows fly;
Life, like a dome of many-colored glass,
Stains the white radiance of Eternity.

The Resurrection

I know that my redeemer liveth, and that he shall stand at the latter day upon the earth.

Job 19:25

And when the sabbath was past, Mary Magdalene, and Mary the mother of James, and Salome, had bought sweet spices, that they might come and anoint him. And very early in the morning the first day of the week, they came unto the sepulchre at the rising of the sun. And they said among themselves, Who shall roll us away the stone from the door of the sepulchre? And when they looked, they saw that the stone was rolled away: for it was very great. And entering into the sepulchre, they saw a young man sitting on the right side, clothed in a long white garment; and they were affrighted. And he saith unto them, Be not affrighted: Ye seek Jesus of Nazareth, which was crucified; he is risen; he is not here: behold the place where they laid him. But go your way, tell his disciples and Peter that he goeth before you into Galilee: there shall ye see him, as he said unto you.

Mark 16:1-7

Comfort ye, comfort ye my people, saith your God.

Isaiah 40:1

For he is like a refiner's fire . . . and he shall purify. . . .

Malachi 3:2-3

Then the same day at evening, being the first day of the week, when the doors were shut where the disciples were assembled for fear of the Jews, came Jesus and stood in the midst, and saith unto them, Peace be unto you. And when he had so said, he shewed unto them his hands, and his side. Then were the disciples glad, when they saw the Lord.

John 20:19-20

REJOICE GREATLY, O DAUGHTER OF ZION: shout, O daughter of Jerusalem: behold, thy King cometh unto thee.

Zechariah 9:9

THROUGH MY WINDOW

Pamela Kennedy

And as they came out, they found a man of Cyrene, Simon by name: him they compelled to bear his cross.

Matthew 27:32

It was early in the morning when Simon left the home of his friends and bid good-by to his sons, Rufus and Alexander. He was determined to get to Jerusalem early and discover for himself the truth about the young teacher so many claimed to be the Messiah. It was a lot of rubbish, he felt; another religious zealot who had captured the fancies of the common folk with a few magic tricks and some well-turned phrases. Normally, Simon would not be concerned with such a man, but he felt compelled to examine this itinerant preacher because of the interest of his sons.

For years Simon had instructed his two young sons in the traditions of the Jewish law. He had taught them from the sacred writings of the prophets and saved his earnings for the time when they were both old enough to be brought to Jerusalem for the Passover. Early in the year, he and the two boys, young men now, had set out on the long journey from their Cyrenian home on the North African coast. They traveled along the southern shores of the Mediterranean, through the northern reaches of Egypt, up into the land of Judea, to the city of Jerusalem. They had made arrangements to stay with an old family friend who had land in the countryside.

Soon after their arrival, Alexander and Rufus became fascinated with the teachings of a young Jew named Jesus. Every day they sought out other followers of this teacher and trailed along after them wherever they went. It was nothing to be bothered with, Simon had thought, until they began to bring home tales of miraculous healings, of thousands fed from meager supplies, and even of dead men coming back to life.

It was this last claim that had convinced Simon to seek out Jesus himself and put an end to the foolish rumors his sons kept carrying home. He had brought them to Jerusalem to partake in their faith and heritage, not to be led astray by some heretic.

As he walked along the dusty road, Simon rehearsed the questions he would put to the young man. They were questions that would certainly show Jesus for the fraud he was.

Nearing the gate of the city, Simon stepped to the side of the road to let the jostling crowds pass. There was an unusual number of people hurrying out of the gate for this time of day, he thought. Then, through the clamor of the crowd, Simon heard the unmistakable sound of soldiers marching in cadence, leather and steel creaking and clashing. Dust rose in the hot air, glistening in the sun. Then a sound like mourning reached Simon—low moaning and murmuring as dozens of voices blended together in one sad wail. Simon pushed back to the road's edge to get a better view.

As he watched the approaching procession, Simon noticed two Roman officers studying him. Suddenly, they left their fellows and strode purposefully toward Simon. The one on the right pulled his flat sword from its scabbard and laid it heavily upon Simon's shoulder. His mouth went dry and his heart pounded in his ears. Although he was from Cyrene, he knew the implication of the soldier's gesture. In Roman-occupied Jerusalem, an officer of the occupying forces had only to tap a Jew on the shoulder in order to compel him to perform the most menial or degrading of tasks. The Jew had no choice other than death if he refused to comply.

Yanking him roughly by the cloak, the officer pulled Simon to the center of the dusty road. "Pick up the cross and carry it for this weakling," the Roman snarled as he pushed Simon to the dust next to a dirty, bleeding man. Faced with no alternative, Simon hastened to lift the heavy beam from the shoulders of the criminal. As he did so, the beaten man raised himself to his knees, then struggled to his feet. He stood before Simon, looking into his eyes, and for Simon the look was like a searing flame which burned his very soul. Time and noise and all else seemed to cease and there was only the man and the eyes in all the world. Through his dry lips, Simon managed a hoarse whisper, "Who are you?" and the man answered in a voice that spoke more to Simon's heart than to his ears. "I am Jesus." In that instant it was as if all his questions were answered, not with words but with understanding.

Simon turned and began the long climb up the hill named Golgotha, bearing the cross upon which Jesus would soon be crucified. His heart ached with every step as Simon began to see what his sons had come to understand. The words of the prophet Isaiah echoed in his memory:

"But he was wounded for our transgressions, he was bruised for our iniquities: the chastisement of our peace was upon him; and with his stripes we are healed."

Simon turned his head and glanced backward at the stumbling Messiah. Daring the Roman guard's lash, he called in a barely audible whisper, "Is it you, Lord? Are you the long awaited One?"

Jesus raised his head and captured Simon's eyes with his own once more. Exhaustion and pain were there, but something even more compelling than these—pity and love. Slowly, almost imperceptibly, he nodded in reply. Simon's heart leapt. It was true, then. All the prophecies were to be fulfilled. Yes, there was tragedy and sorrow at the cross, but the plan of Jehovah would not be thwarted. All the promises would be realized. Simon did not know how God would work, but he had a faith greater than his sight—and a God he knew to be far greater than death.

Pamela Kennedy is a freelance writer of short stories, articles, essays, and children's books. Married to a naval officer and mother of three children, she has made her home on both U.S. coasts and currently resides in Hawaii. She draws her material from her own experiences and memories, adding bits of imagination to create a story or mood.

Break Forth into Joy

How beautiful upon the mountains are the feet of him that bringeth good tidings, that publisheth peace; that bringeth good tidings of good, that publisheth salvation; that saith unto Zion, Thy God reigneth!

Isaiah 52:7

For as the heavens are higher than the earth, so are my ways higher than your ways, and my thoughts than your thoughts.

Isaiah 55:9

For as the rain cometh down, and the snow from heaven, and returneth not thither, but watereth the earth, and maketh it bring forth and bud, that it may give seed to the sower, and bread to the eater: so shall my word be that goeth forth out of my mouth.

For ye shall go out with joy, and be led forth with peace: the mountains and the hills shall break forth before you into singing, and all the trees of the field shall clap their hands. Instead of the thorn shall come up the fir tree, and instead of the brier shall come up the myrtle tree: and it shall be to the Lord for a name, for an everlasting sign that shall not be cut off.

Isaiah 55:10-13

Break forth into joy, sing together, ye waste places of Jerusalem: for the Lord hath comforted his people, he hath redeemed Jerusalem.

Isaiah 52:9

Lift up your heads, O ye gates; and be ye lift up, ye everlasting doors; and the King of glory shall come in.

Psalm 24:7

Photo Opposite
THE CHAPEL OF THE HOLY CROSS
SEDONA, ARIZONA
Bob Clemenz Photography

The Bells of Easter

Dolores Cains

Easter bells ring out at dawn
Their message o'er the way.
They tell us of the risen Christ
Who dwells in us today.

As sunlight floods the valley
And tips the trees with gold,
Their joyful music fills the air
As Easter's story is told.

The melodies of love and hope
Peal out so sweet and clear
And bring a quiet peacefulness
To all of those who hear.

And when the tunes are ended
And the last note fades away,
We find our hearts uplifted
On this glad Easter Day.

Church of My Childhood

Carice Williams

The little old church of my childhood
Is bright in my mind once again;
Its pews overflowing each Sunday
With worshipping women and men.

I can hear those sweet voices, like angels,
Resounding to heaven above,
As the righteous were whispering softly
Petitions of praise and of love.

I have frequently thought of the numbers
Of prayers that were uttered with zeal,
And I'm back in the church of my childhood
As the old chapel bells start to peal.

Photo Overleaf
MISSION SANTA BARBARA
SANTA BARBARA, CALIFORNIA
Dick Dietrich

COUNTRY CHRONICLE

Lansing Christman

I never fail to participate in two Easter Sunday services: one in the out-of-doors, and another in the country church. For the service at sunrise, I go to the sanctuary of the hills. There I look and listen, absorbing all I can of nature and spring as I ponder the greatness of the universe.

I celebrate the promise of eternal life as the rays of the morning sun rise above the eastern horizon. I celebrate the rebirth and renewal so evident in what I see and hear. I behold God's gift of sun and song, bulb and bloom, of stirring seed and sprout.

After the sunrise ritual, I go to the old country church nestled in the foothills of the Blue Ridge. Spring has graced the landscape with the splendor of peach tree blossoms.

The Gothic architecture of the church, based on churches built centuries ago in Western Europe, is an imposing array of ribbed vaulting, pointed arches, flying buttresses, steep roofs, and a lofty steeple pointing to the heavens above. Its beauty is majestic to behold.

The stained glass windows of the sanctuary portray the major events in the ministry of Christ. As I listen to the hymns of praise and the messages of Easter, I continue my celebration of the Resurrection. My spiritual needs, this glorious day, are satisfied. There is the promise, the reassurance of life without end.

The author of two published books, Lansing Christman has been contributing to Ideals *for almost twenty years. Mr. Christman has also been published in several American, foreign, and braille anthologies. He and his wife, Lucile, live in rural South Carolina where they enjoy the pleasures of the land around them.*

Awe of April

Gertrude Rudberg

I stood upon a windswept hill,
The world beneath my feet,
And watched the birth of spring come in
As winter took retreat.

I saw beyond the countryside,
Its spread of emerald green,
The naked trees all budded out
In leaves of silken sheen.
I saw a willow tree bent low
In skirts of yellow grace,
And overhead the heavens blue
were stitched in ribboned lace.

I saw below a rivulet
Singing in ecstasy,
And all along its winding path
Was ice, now broken free.

I stood and looked far, far away
Across the waking earth,
And felt within a deep response
To April and new birth.

Photo Opposite
WILDFLOWERS BENEATH A PALOVERDE TREE
ORGANPIPE CACTUS NATIONAL MONUMENT
Harry Jarvis

Brother and Sister

Edith Shaw Butler

They always brought the cows home
From pasture every night.
Their eyes and ears were open
To every sound and sight.

He hushed for sudden peepings;
She searched for lily bells;
A child's heart in April
Knows many magic spells.

They picked the first spring flowers:
Hepaticas of blue,
And vowed to make a secret
Of the thicket where they grew.

They learned the world together,
The bitter and the sweet,
And knew the joy of springtime,
Immeasurable, complete.

There Was a Child Went Forth

Walt Whitman

There was a child
went forth every day,
And the first object
that he looked upon,
that object he became,
And that object
became part of him
for the day
or a certain part of the day,
Or for many years
or stretching cycles of years.

Ivan's Easter Service

Amelia W. Swayne

Ivan was a little Russian boy who lived in the city of St. Petersburg. It was the day before Easter, and he was very happy because he was to be allowed to go to the great church for the midnight service. His sister, Sonia, who was older than he was, had gone the year before and remembered much of what had happened.

As they set out from their home, Ivan asked, "Why is the church so dark when we go in?"

"Because people are remembering the time when everyone thought Jesus was dead," said his mother.

"That was a very dark time," said his father. "People thought the light of the world had gone out. The darkness of the church is to remind us of that time."

Soon they came to the church. As they went in, each one was given a candle. Ivan carried his very carefully and sat down quietly beside his father. He could hear the soft music, but he could not see the great organ. Up on the altar a low light burned. The priest was beginning the service. He sang many parts of it, and the choir replied from time to time. Ivan could not understand all they were saying, but the music was very beautiful, and he was glad to be sitting there close to his father.

The priest finished his prayer and, with the other priests and the choir, walked down the aisle. Ivan could hear the swish of their robes as they passed him. They left the church, and now all was very, very quiet and very, very dark. Ivan sat as still as he could and tried to think how the world would be if no one remembered the things that Jesus had taught.

Suddenly the great bells rang out, and the whole church seemed to become full of light. Easter Day had come! The priests and choir marched in singing joyfully, "He is risen," and everyone seemed very happy. A priest held out a shining taper, and Ivan reached up to it to light his candle. He now saw that the church was crowded with people all lighting candles. Soon after they had done this, the service ended, and everyone started home carrying his light carefully.

"Christ is risen!" said Ivan's father.

"He is risen indeed!" replied his mother.

"Christ is risen!" said Sonia.

"He is risen indeed!" said Ivan.

Ivan was very happy. He was glad that he had gone to the church. He was glad that he could carry home his bright candle.

"It would still be dark if we were not carrying our lights, wouldn't it?" he said.

from *A Child's Story of Easter,*
published by Ideals Publishing Corporation,
Nashville, Tennessee 37214

A Slice of Life

Edgar A. Guest

They seldom show Him with a smile.
   Always His face is sad to see,
   As if a jest could never be
Nor He be merry for a while.
The kindly humor that could pat
   The brows of boys He chanced to see
   And say: "Let children come to me!"
No brush has ever pictured that!

The man who loved a little child
   And walked the common ways of men,
   Though troubled often, now and then
With those about Him surely smiled.
I fancy as I read His word
   I hear Him chuckling, soft and sweet,
   Telling to Mary, at His feet,
Some curious thing He'd seen or heard.

He must have had a twinkling eye,
   Which danced at times with gentle mirth,
   So greatly to be loved on earth,
So bravely on the cross to die.

Edgar A. Guest joined the staff of the Detroit Free Press *at the age of fourteen. He was a regular contributor of verse and humorous sketches to the* Chicago Tribune *and the author of numerous volumes of popular verse.*

All Things Bright and Beautiful

Cecil F. Alexander

All things bright and beautiful,
All creatures great and small,
All things wise and wonderful,
The Lord God made them all.

Each little flower that opens,
Each little bird that sings,
He made their glowing colors,
He made their tiny wings.

The cold wind in the winter,
The pleasant summer rain,
The ripe fruits in the garden,
He made them every one.

The tall trees in the greenwood,
The meadows where we play,
The rushes by the water
We gather every day;

He gave us eyes to see them,
And lips that we might tell
How great is God Almighty,
Who has made all things well.

Photo Opposite
BABY GIRL WATERING GARDEN
Vision Impact

Spring Tonic

Catherine E. Jackson

First place one jonquil in your hands;
Inhale its fragrance deeply;
Then buy one redbird's little song;
(You'll find they come quite cheaply).
When ready, find the oldest tree
Within your vision growing;
Remain quite still until you feel
The sweet warm breezes blowing.
Now blend these things most tenderly
With young imagination;
And when you finish, you will know
Your soul's rejuvenation!

My Back Door

Loise Pinkerton Fritz

Today God made a rainbow
Without a cloud in sight;
In fact, the sun was shining
And all the world was bright.
The lilacs bloomed profusely,
Perfuming all the air,
And there was music in the breeze,
Birds singing everywhere.

Today God made a rainbow
In such a splendid way.
He fashioned it from sunbeams
And water that I sprayed.
As I hosed down the old back porch,
A humble, homely chore,
He made a lovely rainbow
As close as my back door.

THE PASTURE

Robert Frost

I'm going out to clean the pasture spring;
I'll only stop to rake the leaves away
(And wait to watch the water clear, I may):
I shan't be gone long. — You come too.

I'm going out to fetch the little calf
That's standing by the mother. It's so young,
It totters when she licks it with her tongue.
I shan't be gone long. — You come too.

Photo Opposite
TWO BOYS RUNNING IN STREAM
Vision Impact

Rain

Louis Ginsberg

As I was lying sick in bed,
I heard them patter overhead;
And turning to the window there,
I saw them glitter through the air.
I heard them clinking, clinking plain
And range into a clear refrain—
A million, million drops of rain!

On every blade of grass and tree
The raindrops splashed divinity;
While every crack and every chink
Puts up its eager lips to drink.

My senses, freed from bonds and bars,
Beheld it all a rain of stars
With every drop a blazing sun:
A swift deluging never done
Of music merging into one
With every note of fire spun. . . .

For every rounded drop of rain
Kept ringing clear and clean and plain—
Kept ringing clear again, again,
As if from bells of crystal rolled,
And bells of bronze and bells of gold—
Oh, every big, round drop set chiming
A vast and universal rhyming!

The shower, pouring on my need,
Flooded my heart which was a seed
That, soaking, swelling, bursting, grew
To all the scenes I ever knew:
To meadows brightening in my brain,
To cities flashing in the rain;
Until my heart with a new birth—
My heart became the earth, the earth!

America's Raccoons

Robert A. Weaver

Despite the popularity of Daniel Boone's coonskin cap, raccoons are in abundance in America to both the delight and consternation of their human neighbors. The raccoon, truly an all-American animal, is found in every one of the states but Hawaii. His masked eyes and bushy, striped tail are charming features familiar to children and adults everywhere. If only they weren't so full of mischief. . . .

More intelligent than most small mammals, raccoons are adaptable, forward "bandits", unafraid of entering our world. They are notorious for taking food from campsites, raiding chicken houses, tipping garbage cans, stealing farmers' crops, and even tearing screen doors to get at food left on unattended tables. As nocturnal animals, raccoons perform their mischief at night and sleep during the day in dens which are often marvels of ingenuity. A "coon's" first choice is a hollow log or tree, but he makes do with crates, barrels, garages, barns, and caves. When he can't find any interesting food to pilfer, he fishes from stream banks for crayfish, snails, frogs, or fish. He is known for his cleanliness and washes his food before eating it. The raccoon uses his front paws in much the same manner as we use our hands, making him an endearing fisherman to observe.

The mother raccoon's springtime litter will consist of two to seven babies weighing three ounces each. They are unable to see until they are three weeks old; but by the time they are three months old, the baby raccoons are big enough to learn the art of food-gathering from their experienced and clever mother and make a jolly parade trailing behind her during her nocturnal raids.

Raccoons are related to the bear family and hibernate throughout most of the winter. Now that it is spring again, the raccoons are waking up, having babies, and making their midnight visits to our tantalizing homesteads once again.

Photo Opposite
YOUNG RACCOON
Robert Cushman Hayes

The Waterfall

Angie Davidson Bass

My heart will forever recall, I know,
A day of joy when, long ago,
I walked a trail through fir and pine
And held the forest's breath in mine:
The pure, fresh breath of forest scent
That filled my being with content.

Upon a jutting cliff so steep,
I gazed into the canyon deep
And listened to the mountain call
In thunder through the waterfall,
Where white foam churned against the brink,
And white-tailed deer came down to drink.

I've often walked where rivers stray,
Beside cascades in misty spray,
But I had never hoped to stand
With shimmering rainbows in my hand
As on that day, exalted, tall,
I stood beside a waterfall.

Before Storm

Frances Frost

This wind is the voice of rain
Crossing the hills. Sun,
Hear the rain coming! Hide
In the pines, in the clouds! Run,

Rabbits: flatten your ears
And scurry down to the cool
Arms of the earth. By the shallow,
Reed-shadowed, dusky pool,
Hush your green throats, frogs!
The trees are dark with the stain
Of slanting wetness. Wind,

Though you push the grasses over,
Here is a meadowlark come down
From the cloud to the dripping clover,
And a rabbit at the edge of his burrow,
Delightedly sniffing the rain!

The Fawn

Alexandra Gabriel

We watch him tremble on knobby legs
Like stilts of velvet rust.
He browses, first Mother, then bright sheep sorrel
And fresh spring clover tufts.

He wanders with exquisite, weightless grace
Over deadfall and young columbine,
To a sun-shafted, pine-vaulted clearing:
The forest's cathedral divine.

Glistening with innocence, his nutbrown eyes
Meekly take in the sun.
He blinks at creation—a miracle,
Not knowing that he too is one.

Photo Opposite
WHITE-TAILED FAWN
Len Rue, Jr.
H. Armstrong Roberts, Inc.

Homebuilder

Dorene

Over and under, oh, what can it be
Under and over the white lilac tree?
Down to the ground for a bit of bright thread,
Gracefully up to a branch overhead;
Whirring away for a wisp of a weed,
Back again, weaving with wisdom and speed;
Takeoffs and landings—a hundred or more—
Twigs, leaves, and rootlets flown in by the score.

Up and down, in and out, over and under;
Deftness, precision, amazement, and wonder!
Under and over, oh, what can it be?
A homebuilding brown thrush—*come quickly and see!*

Pied Beauty

Gerard Manley Hopkins

Glory be to God for dappled things—
   For skies of couple-color as a brindled cow;
     For rose-moles all in stipple upon trout that swim;
Fresh-firecoal chestnut-falls; finches wings;
    Landscape plotted and pieced—fold, fallow, and plow;
    And all trades, their gear and tackle and trim.

All things counter, original, spare, strange;
   Whatever is fickle, freckled (who knows how?)
    With swift, slow; sweet, sour; adazzle, dim;
He fathers-forth whose beauty is past change:
          Praise him.

COLLECTOR'S CORNER

Why collect or make miniatures? Probably for much the same reason that Gulliver found himself so fascinated with Lilliput. Homely implements of everyday life become beautiful in miniature scale, and can help us understand more completely the big world in which we live. When I made my first chair, I learned how to appreciate what I had previously taken for granted. To make something look realistic is to see it for the first time.

Miniaturists today draw from a long history which goes all the way back to the Egyptians and Greco-Romans, but the first documented dollhouse was that of Albrecht V, Duke of Bavaria, who commissioned the building for his young daughter in 1558. When finished, he placed it in his art collection. The four-story building reflected the life of the period. The first floor included a stable, cow barn, office, larder, wine cellar, and coach house. The second floor had a bathroom (most unusual for the time period), kitchen, courtyard, and orchard. The third floor exhibited the master bedroom and a ballroom with gold tapestries. The fourth floor revealed a chapel, second bedroom, working room, second kitchen, and the nurseries. Unfortunately, this miniature mansion no longer exists.

From the sixteenth century on, the fascination with miniatures grew. In the twentieth century, three women helped inspire miniaturists' work and collections. The first was England's

Queen Mary, for whom almost 1,500 craftsmen and artists contributed their talents to create what is known as Queen Mary's Doll's House. Presented to her in 1924, the three-story, forty-room mansion includes everything from a complete wine celler and miniature library to working elevators, electrical wiring, and toothbrushes. The house set the standard for excellence in its day, and Windsor Castle is now a popular side trip for many miniaturists visiting England.

Here in America, two fabulous collections make Chicago a miniaturist's Mecca. The older of these is the dramatically displayed Fairy Castle in the Chicago Museum of Science and Industry. Silent film star Coleen Moore involved many of her studio craftsmen and artists in the construction of this miniature fairyland palace. Over 100 workers helped to build the castle, begun in 1928, over a seven-year period. The basic structure is built in sections of aluminum, with the exception of one room which is made of bronze! Visitors to the museum hear Ms. Moore's tape-recorded voice describe the painstaking details of her miniature kingdom, which include intricately wrought furniture and picture frames, murals from beloved fairy tales hand-painted on walls and screens, casques of real jewels, entire silver services, a library of tiny, illustrated books of fairy tales, and a tiny pistol which really shoots!

The collection of sixty-eight American and

European rooms, currently housed at the Art Institute of Chicago, is considered one of the top miniature collections in the world. Created under the guidance of Mrs. James Ward Thorne between 1937 and 1940, these rooms chronicle the history of interior design from the Middle Ages to the 1930s. An attention to detail and authenticity is the hallmark of her rooms. The highest compliment a collector can receive is that his dollhouse is of "Thorne room quality."

Working with a large and mostly anonymous staff, Mrs. Thorne herself researched, arranged, and helped accessorize the rooms. She is said to have made rugs, chandeliers, and other pieces, and even upholstered some of the furniture. She was able to do everything but carve, so the carving and building of the shells for the rooms was done by another Chicago studio, but the finishing was done in her own. In the 1940s, the original ninety-five-room collection was divided up, and the twenty-seven rooms not in Chicago reside in Phoenix, Arizona, and Knoxville, Tennessee.

The scale of the above collections is a one-inch to one-foot ratio. This was the primary scale used up through the 1970s. Today, however, as people run short of display area, smaller scales are gaining in popularity.

Just how many people collect miniatures? One writer estimates that there are 63,000 miniature collectors and crafters, which includes some 3,000 to 4,000 artists and craftsmen.

Many miniaturists create their own houses and settings from scratch—an endeavor which can involve the whole family. Skill at needlework, ceramics, interior design, railroad landscaping, decorative painting, as well as doll-making and model assembly might be required to finish a miniature project.

Anyone interested can find complete mansions ready to finish or furnish, as well as blown glass, elaborately carved Belter furniture, real silver, hand-painted oil paintings, and lacquer ware. Almost any piece of a home can be found: from boxes of cereal to saddles and riding boots; from cats and dogs to miniature floral arrangements; from dressed "people" to working grandfather clocks!

Two of the largest miniature-oriented organizations are the National Association of Miniature Enthusiasts (N.A.M.E.) and the International Guild of Miniature Artisans, Ltd. (I.G.M.A.).

N.A.M.E. was founded in 1972 and currently has 11,800 members throughout the world. N.A.M.E. members attend house parties and conventions, and receive *Miniature Gazette,* a quarterly about their "small world."

I.G.M.A. was established in 1979 to bring together the artists, and more recently, the collectors, dealers, and enthusiasts of miniature art. The current membership of 760 people gathers annually for a show and a week of workshops.

Even non-collectors are charmed by the realism which fine miniaturists achieve in their small-scale replicas of our everyday world. Looking into a dollhouse, something attracts us to pull up a tiny chair, put up our feet on a tiny footstool, thumb through a tiny book, and dream away.

Charles Claudon

Charles Claudon is Second Vice-President of N.A.M.E. and is an artisan of I.G.M.A. He makes miniatures and owns the Butterfly Cat Studio in Park Forest, Illinois.

To a Chipmunk

Don Thorne

Go, make your chitter-chatter
At some other open door.
The fact is, in this old house,
You are not welcome anymore.
You have become a pest, you know,
You've overstayed your leave.
Your *elan* was my undoing:
You led me to believe
That you were wise and prudent
In ways of world and man.
Now go away, and stay away;
You've lost an avid fan.

Plug up the down spout . . .
There was a master's stroke!
Nibble on a bag of flour . . .
You almost smothered when it broke!
Tip over plants, fall in my milk,
Break lamps and dishes too.
Sometimes I think your only dream
Is mischief you can do.
Inventor of catastrophes,
Now go your noisy way!
Go, flick your tail,
Scoot out the door,
And chatter life away!
No more of you! The door is shut!
Go pester Jay and Wren!
. . . Come back some day,
I suppose I'll smile . . .
And let you in again.

Photo Overleaf
HOUSE AND TULIPS
WILLIAMSBURG, VIRGINIA
Gene Ahrens

L'envoi

Rudyard Kipling

When Earth's last picture is painted, and the tubes are
    twisted and dried,
When the oldest colors have faded, and the youngest
    critic has died,
We shall rest, and, faith, we shall need it—lie down
    for an eon or two,
Till the Master of All Good Workmen shall put us to
    work anew.

And those that were good shall be happy: they shall
    sit in a golden chair;
They shall splash at a ten-league canvas with brushes
    of comets' hair;
They shall find real saints to draw from—Magdalene,
    Peter, and Paul;
They shall work for an age at a sitting, and never be
    tired at all!

And only the Master shall praise us, and only the
    Master shall blame;
And no one shall work for money, and no one shall
    work for fame;
But each for the joy of the working, and each, in his
    separate star,
Shall draw the Thing as he sees It for the *God of
Things as They Are!*

Spring Meadow

Louis Ginsberg

Butterflies rejoice to be
Documenting deity.

Slipping testament, each goes,
Reassured at every rose.

Every eager bough is bent,
Verifying sacrament.

Learning clearness from on high,
Little pools rehearse the sky.

Old in quiet wisdom, trees
Sink their roots in verities.

Birds, that chirrup in the hum,
Pivot on delirium;

While the daisies dramatize
Constellations of the skies.

Readers' Forum

I am one of your readers and have been so for years. I cannot think of any finer gift to send to my friends who can read English. . . . Thank you for publishing such a beautiful publication.

Ms. Gurly Shiffert
Vastervik, Sweden

I enjoy the readers' comments at the back of the current issues. I certainly agree with them in their enthusiastic appreciation of Ideals. I "discovered" Ideals way back in the early '50s and am as pleased with each new issue as I was then. Long may you be there to keep on publishing such a beautiful and inspiring magazine.

Jenn E. Hauser
Erie, PA

I would like to compliment you on printing such a beautiful magazine. I have been receiving subscriptions for over twenty-five years, . . . and this magazine has really been an inspiration to me in my work. . . . I am a disabled artist, and since my physical limitations have prevented me from taking my work out into the field, I have used the beautiful photographs in Ideals for many of my subjects. . . . My sincere thanks for this wholesome and beautiful publication. . . .

Nancy Quinn
St. Petersburg, FL

I wish to extend my sincere THANKS for publishing a beautiful poetry book. I am presently an Activity Director for a Senior Housing project in the Austin area and use the books on a regular basis. The only complaint I have is: Why don't you issue one for St. Patrick's Day? I am just a "wee bit blessed with some Irish in me" and would like to see poems about the Irish.

Maureen L. Cahill
Austin, MN

Ideals *has been through a lot with me, and whenever I feel blue or really sad I pick up an* Ideals *and I feel comforted. They are wonderful and moral and give me faith that there is good in this world.*

Mrs. Marian Fischer
Cohocton, NY

I call my Ideals my "Happiness Book" after looking through other magazines and seeing so many pages about grief, sickness, and loneliness. I don't need those things. Being seventy years old, I need a magazine like yours—one that shares happiness.

Ms. Sue L. Tallent
Madisonville, TN

I receive Ideals on a regular basis as a gift from a very dear friend. This is one publication that I always look forward to receiving.

Mrs. Ann L. Chapman
Aiken, SC

* * *

CRAFTWORKS

Readers are invited to submit original craft ideas for possible development and publication in future *Ideals* issues. Please send query letter with idea (and photograph, if available) to "Craftworks," Ideals Publishing Corporation, P.O. Box 140300, Nashville, Tennessee 37214-0300. Do not send samples; they cannot be returned.

Upon acceptance, writers must supply design, text instructions, and sample product. Payment will vary accordingly and will be upon publication.

ideals

Celebrating Life's Most Treasured Moments